VASSILY BRANDT
ETUDES FOR TRUMPET
(Orchestra Etudes and Last Etudes)

Edited by William Vacchiano

The *Etudes for Trumpet* consists of two series of study material for trumpet: the *Orchestra Etudes* and the *Last Etudes*. Among students of the instrument, both of these series have met with the most enthusiastic acclaim. There are few instrumental studies which have excited such general enthusiasm and proved so useful in the development of trumpet technique.

The *Orchestra Etudes* reveal the most penetrating insight by the composer into the problems of orchestral technique for the trumpet player. Brandt takes excerpts from the trumpet parts of well-known orchestral scores and develops them skillfully into study material. Among the excerpts to be found are the trumpet parts from Beethoven's *Leonore Overture*, Wagner's *Wedding March* from *Lohengrin*, Tchaikovsky's *Pathétique*, and the *Cappriccio Italien*, Rimsky-Korsakoff's *Scheherazade*, and other much-performed orchestral compositions.

The *Last Etudes* are composed largely of modulating scales. Careful study by the trumpet player will give him unusual mastery of the technique of transposition. The indicated transpositions refer to the desired concert pitch; the exercises should, therefore, be transposed one whole tone higher than indicated. Thus, an indication "in Eb" requires a transposition of a perfect fourth up.

Both series of etudes are for the advanced student and offer invaluable material for the study of phrasing and for warm-up drills.

WILLIAM VACCHIANO

Copyright © 1945 UNIVERSAL MUSIC CORP.
Copyright Renewed
All Rights Reserved   Used by Permission

ETUDES FOR TRUMPET

ORCHESTRA ETUDES

Compiled and Edited by
WILLIAM VACCHIANO

VASSILY BRANDT

1

Suggested Phrasing:

Copyright © 1945 UNIVERSAL MUSIC CORP.
Copyright Renewed
All Rights Reserved   Used by Permission

2

3

4

5

8

9

10

11

Leonora Signal

ff

rall.

12

Alla Polacca

13

15

Allegro grazioso

17

18

19

20

21

Allegro grazioso

22

23

Alla Polacca

24

25

Allegretto

26

27

28

tu tu ku tu tu ku tu tu ku tu tu ku

29

30

31

33

34

LAST ETUDES

1

2

3

4

5

in E♭

6

Fine

D.C. al Fine

8

in A, Bb, C

9

10

in F, E

in F, E

14

in Eb, D

15

in Eb, D

16

17

18

19

21

23

24